Is Halloween Yet?

by Jon Lymon

A rhyming tale of a shy ghost
who's scared of frightening people

Is It
Halloween
Yet?

Is It Halloween Yet?

by Jon Lymon

A rhyming tale of a shy ghost
who's scared of frightening people

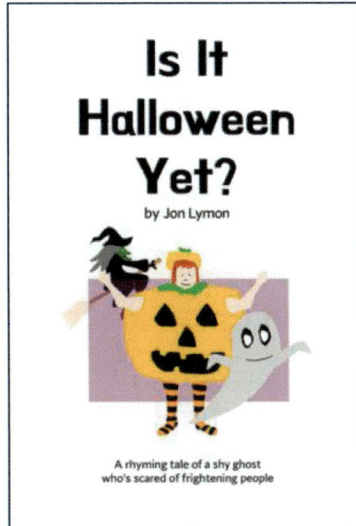

This book is a work of fiction, and any resemblance to actual persons, living or dead, is purely coincidental.

This book is sold subject to the condition that it shall not be lent, resold, hired out, or otherwise circulated without the author's consent.

1

Ghouella the ghost was frightened of being scary

She didn't like making people jump out of their skin

So she hid herself away in cold, dark places

Hardly daring to show her face or make a sound from within

But there was one day of the year she didn't have to hide

And that day was Halloween

But with no wrist for a watch nor pocket for a phone

How would she know when it was safe to be seen?

As Ghouella hid, she listened carefully and wondered

When will it be Halloween?

Will she guess right, and come out without giving fright?

You're about to find out, so let's see

2

Ghouella heard the scrape of many sticks

Along a polished oak wooden floor

'Is it Halloween yet?' she wondered

Was that a witch's broom about to soar?

She blew open the
door behind which
she'd been hiding

And gave a poor
cleaner such a
terrible fright

He dropped his
brush, and off
he rushed

Before Ghouella
could try and put
things right

$$x^2 = y$$

Ghouella looked around the empty classroom

And hunched her shoulders in disappointment and despair

It definitely wasn't Halloween time yet

And she'd really given that school cleaner a scare

So she drifted away through a crack in the ceiling

To find somewhere else

where she could stay and safely hide

And wait for Halloween to come along

When she could come out

and be herself with pride

3

A knocking sound disturbed Ghouella this time

There it was, an unmistakable tap on a door

Is it Halloween yet? she wondered

Was it trick or treaters? She had to see more

So she slid through a gap in the dark place she'd been hiding

And found herself in a room full of children

With grown-ups at the door dropping off a few kids more

Birthday presents piling up on a table beside them

When they saw Ghouella, the partygoers screamed
Parents dragged their children out of the room
Some said 'beg your pardon' and ran into the garden
Leaving poor Ghouella alone in the gloom

'Come back, come back,' she wanted to say

But no one was there to hear her words

Ghouella had thought she'd heard some Halloween fun

The way they'd all reacted just seemed so absurd

4

Ghouella was awoken by the sound of much laughter

Was that a witch's ear-splitting shriek?

'Is it Halloween yet?' she wondered as more laughter thundered

She had to take a quick peek

The woman who'd been laughing looked right at Ghouella

And screamed and screeched so very very loud

Ghouella could see she wasn't a witch at all

Just a mum sitting with her kids among the crowd

At the wonderful, colourful, magical circus

With clowns fooling around in the ring

But now their audience was all running away

From the ghost they couldn't believe they'd just seen

The clowns saw Ghouella, and their smiles disappeared

They grabbed their jackets and hats and then fled

Leaving Ghouella to strop alone in the big top

All the fun gone, her heart full of dread

5

'Is it Halloween yet?' Ghouella wondered

hearing splishing and splashing

That must be people apple bobbing, she thought

I'll take a look and see what I'm missing

I wonder how many juicy fruits they've caught

She walked through a set of sliding glass doors

Out onto people laughing in a swimming pool of fun

Smiling turned to screaming when they saw Ghouella gleaming

Floating while her flowing cape reflected the sun

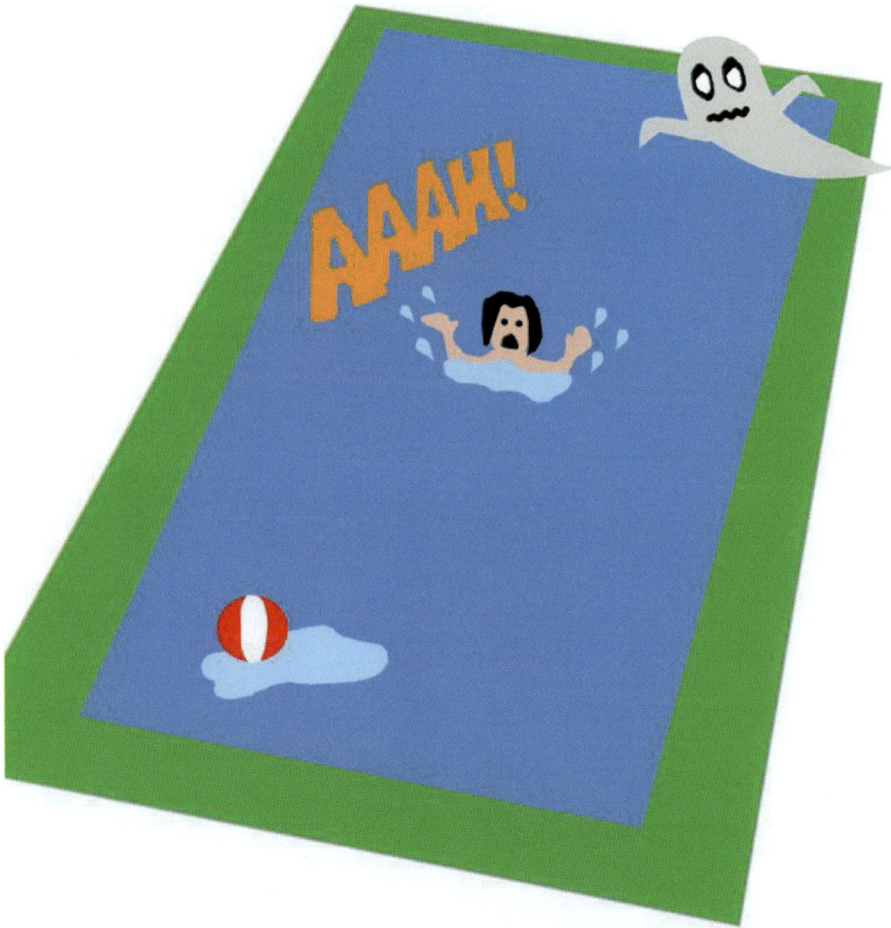

Swimmers jumped out, grabbed their towels and ran

Leaving Ghouella by the water alone

With the sun so hot, she knew it definitely was not

Halloween time - it was time for her to go

She squeezed through a hole in a fence by the pool

And drifted away into a big dark wood

Wondering if it would ever be Halloween again

The time of year she could be herself and feel good

6

'Is it Halloween yet?' Ghouella wondered

hearing screeching and scraping

Could it be a witch stirring a huge cauldron of green?

Or was it a wicked spell she was making

or something else she was baking?

Ghouella had to find out and risk being seen

Ghouella drifted out of the dark place she'd been hiding

And found herself high up, just beneath the fluffy clouds

On a building site among the dust and scaffolding

With men in hard hats working around and about

Some looked up and couldn't believe what they were seeing

Was that a ghost among the bricks, metal and wood?

None wanted to hang around, they all started to climb down

Rushing off the building site as fast as they could

'Don't go,' called Ghouella. 'I just want to talk
All this ghouling around is far from thrilling'
But the builders didn't hear, they all wanted her to disappear
So they could get back to their hammering and drilling

7

Ghouella heard the sound of hissing and booing

Is it Halloween yet? it made her wonder

Was it ghosts saying boo to frighten a human or two

She needed to find out, so slipped out from where she was under

She squeezed her way through a gap in some steps

And hovered above a really large football crowd

Whose team was being attacked, a mistake by the left back

Led to an own goal that made them boo louder

But the boos of those fans quickly turned to yells and screams

As they saw Ghouella rise up right before their eyes

Some fans jumped out of their seats, others decided to leap

Onto the pitch still grasping their half-time meat pies

'Where are you all going?' a desperate Ghouella cried out
'I'm only here because I thought you all were ghosts'
But by now the game had stopped and the players had gone off
Most fans were running, others clinging to the goalposts

8

Ghouella was finished, she'd given up all hope

Of ever finding the fun of Halloween

Every time she thought it was here, it soon became clear

She was wrong and just making people scream

So when she heard boos and laughter, splashing and scraping

She decided to stay hiding exactly where she was

But someone opened the door and yelled out some more

Seeing Ghouella hiding amid the brushes and mops

'Don't be scared', Ghouella cried to the person outside

But then something happened that was really quite amazing

The person just smiled, and said the fright had been wild

'Come join the party, we're going Halloween crazy'

Ghouella was unsure as she glided through the door

Until she saw bobbing apples and the stirring of spells

No one looked at her and shrieked, or made her feel like a freak

They let her join in their games without even a yell

Ghouella didn't need to ask if it was Halloween yet

She knew this was the time she'd been searching for so long

The day she didn't have to hide, she could enjoy herself outside

Without being thought of as scary and wrong

The End

See more children's books
by Jon Lymon at
jonlymonkidsbooks.com

MORE RHYMING PICTURE BOOKS

THE APPVENTURERS

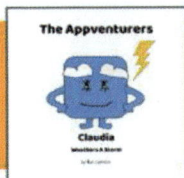 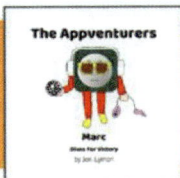 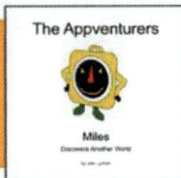 

LONGER READS

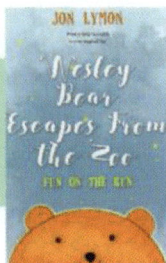 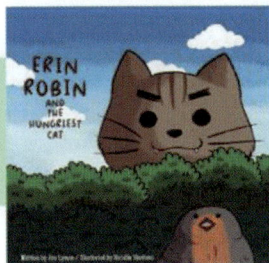 

Printed in Dunstable, United Kingdom